Why Crocodiles Smile

Cric Croc discovers nature's wonders

Anthony W Buirchell • Laila Savolainen

Copyright © 2017
The moral right of Anthony W. Buirchell be identified as the Author and Laila Savolainen as the Artist of the work has been asserted by them in accordance with the Copyright, Designs and Patents Act 1988. All rights reserved. No part of this book may be used or reproduced, stored in a retrieval system, or transmitted in any form, or by any means electronic, mechanical, recording, photocopying, or in any manner whatsoever without permission in writing from the publisher, except for the inclusion of brief quotations in a review.

National Library of Australia Cataloguing-in-Publication entry
Creator: Buirchell, Anthony W., author
Title: Why crocodiles smile, Cric Croc discovers nature's wonders / Anthony Buirchell ;
    Laila Savolainen, illustrator.
ISBN: 978-0-9954243-4-0 (paperback)
    978-0-9954243-5-7 (hardcover)
Series: Buirchell, Anthony W. Cric Croc series ; bk. 3.
Target Audience: For pre-school age
Subjects: Crocodiles-Juvenile fiction. Ponies-Juvenile fiction.
Other Creators/Contributors: Savolainen, Laila, illustrator.

Publishing Details
Published in Australia – Cric Croc Enterprises
www.anthonybuirchell.com

Publishing Consultants
Design and artwork supplied: Pickawoowoo Publishing Group

Printed & Channel Distribution
Lightning Source / Ingram

This book is dedicated to all the children of the World who will fall in love with reading and the excitement it brings.

It is also dedicated to the many nature educators who offer positive, practical experiences for children so they appreciate the unique flora and fauna on our fragile Earth. They are creating children of the future who appreciate nature and will become protectors of all living things.
- AWB

Cric was feeling a little sad. His dad, Crisis asked what was wrong.

"May I visit my family who live in the Daintree?"

Crisis said, "I'll talk to my friend who runs the Daintree River Cruises and ask him if you can stay. He will show you all the unique flora and fauna that live in the Daintree."

So it came about that Cric spent a wonderful week on the Daintree.

He felt the magic of the place and saw lots of colourful birds but ...

When he got home he hugged his dad Crisis and said, "Dad I had a great time but can you tell me why crocodiles smile?"

"Settle in and I'll tell you why."

The bull Crocodile was a sneaky beast
It was looking for a scrumptious feast.
With big yellow eyes it searched around
Looking for food from the watery surround.

The black Cassowary with horn on its head
Looking for food so its chicks could be fed.
Drummed loudly and ran without delay
When the crocodile smiled and looked its way.

The majestic Brolga on its long, long legs
Fossicked and dug for tiny dregs.
Flapped its wings and flew without delay
When the crocodile smiled and looked its way.

The black, long-necked Cormorant dried its wings
Happily sunning after a feed of fingerlings.
Climbed quickly higher without delay
When the crocodile smiled and looked its way.

A sleek, silver Barramundi swimming along.
The river was deep and it wanted to belong.
Swished its tail and dived without delay
When the crocodile smiled and looked its way.

The white, Great Egret paddled in the shallow
Noticed little minnows swimming far below.
Took flight on its long wings without delay
When the crocodile smiled and looked its way.

The Azure Kingfisher ducking and diving
Looking for any fish for its surviving.
Flittered on fast wings without delay
When the crocodile smiled and looked its way.

The Nankeen Night Heron saw the
morning light
It had been hunting all through the night.
Flew off to safety without delay
When the crocodile smiled and looked its way.

The black and white Magpie Geese winged in low
Looking for quiet water far down below.
Glided passed the monster without delay
When the crocodile smiled and looked their way.

The Papuan Frogmouth sat still in the green.
It was so clever to look like the scene.
It stayed still and invisible without delay
When the crocodile smiled and looked its way.

The Striated Heron waded in the mud
Seeking any prey brought down by the flood.
It beat its wings furiously without delay
When the crocodile smiled and looked its way.

A flock of Radjah Ducks swam with webbed feet
Looking for anything they could eat.
They paddled strongly and without delay
When the crocodile smiled and looked their way.

A pair of Fig Parrots chatting without a care
Stripping the fig tree almost bare
Flew away smartly without delay
When the crocodile smiled and looked their way

A pair of raucous Rainbow Lorikeets
Performing wondrous aerial feats
Flittered off noisily without delay
When the crocodile smiled and looked their way

The heavy gliding Pelican away from the sea.
It wasn't as alert as it should be.
It saw the crocodile smile and swim its way.
It was to be dinner this sunny day.

If you enjoyed this book, your family will be delighted by the other books in the Cric Croc Series. Go to www.criccroc.com
Also by Anthony W Buirchell

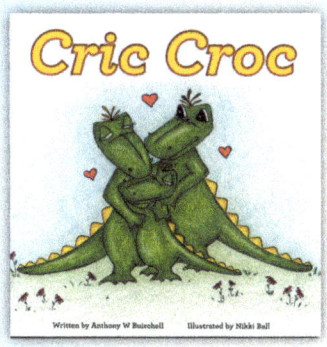 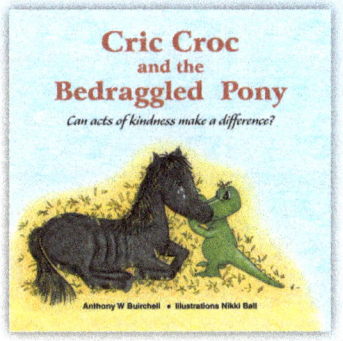

Cric Croc

A concept book based on a baby crocodile learning to lead a healthy life with exercise, good food, plenty of sleep, lots of fun, friends and love. Cric Croc is a role model for good behaviour for children.

Paperback ISBN 9781925442595

Cric Croc and the Bedraggled Pony

Brings into focus kindness, friendship and bullying when Cric Croc finds a bedraggled pony and offers him the help he needs to overcome adversity and thus triumph. The focus is looking beyond the physical appearance to the inner person beneath and how mutual respect and teamwork can be win-win.

Paperback ISBN 9780995424302
Hardcover ISBN 9780995424357

**Cric Croc Visits Schools, Playgroups, After-school care
(Perth Metro)
Bookings www.criccroc.com**

www.ingramcontent.com/pod-product-compliance
Lightning Source LLC
Chambersburg PA
CBHW061932290426
44113CB00024B/2881